Cyber Time Tracker

Book 5

Codey Battles the Botnet

Written by
Jayme Simmons

Cyber Time Tracker: Codey Battles the Botnet

ISBN: 978-1-972486-00-9

Written by Jayme Simmons

Published by ChronoCipher Media

Second Edition

Illustrations created with the assistance of AI tools.

Printed in the United States of America

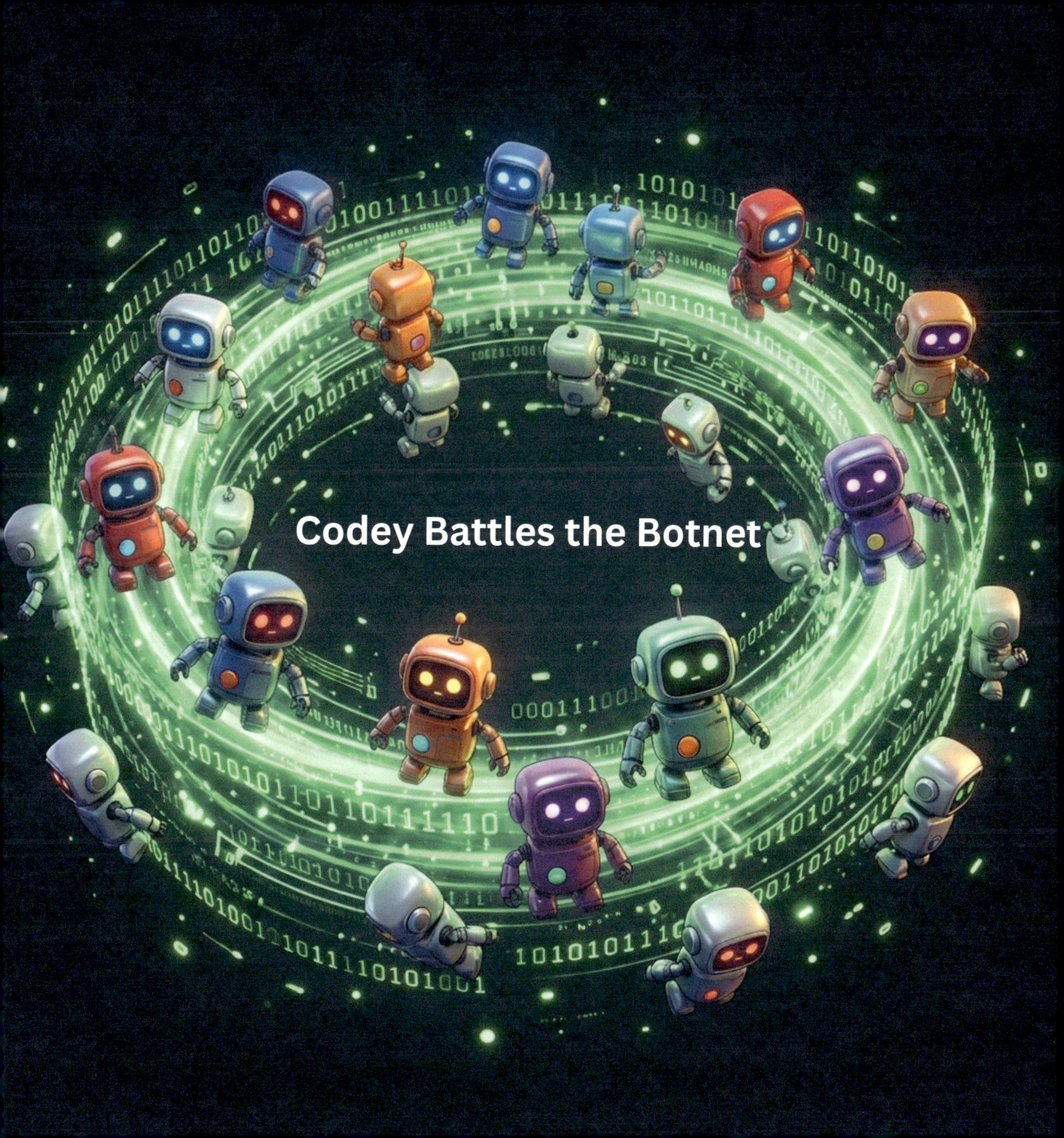
Codey Battles the Botnet

Codey set the ChronoCipher hourglass
gently on his desk.

It was quiet.
Balanced.
Normal.

Almost.

One tiny grain inside drifted upward, glowing green.
Then another.

Across the room, his smart lamp flicked on.
Off. Then on again.

Codey blinked.
"Okay... that's not a feature." He glanced around.

"Cypher?" Nothing answered.

"I didn't touch anything," he added, just in case.

The green grains multiplied.

Binary bent sideways.

Time stuttered, not forward, not back.

Every device in the room blinked once.

Together.

Cypher's voice lowered.

"That's the problem," she said.

"The devices are acting as one."

She paused.

"Like a single mind of a zombie army of robots."

The ChronoCipher flared bright green.

The house went quiet.

Too quiet.

The ChronoCipher stayed still on Codey's desk.

No spinning.

No jumping.

The room glowed soft and sleepy. Then,

Codey's nightlight blinked.

His toy robot's eyes dimmed, then brightened.

Codey tilted his head.

"Okay," he said. "That's... new."

Cypher's voice was calm.

"Little problems grow when no one fixes them," she said.

Codey and Cypher decided to see if there was

anything else acting weird in the house.

They went to the living room.

The TV flashed, then went dark.

It wouldn't connect to the internet.

Codey held up a nearby tablet

and tapped the screen.

It didn't respond right away.

Same flash.

Same pause.

Codey squinted.

"Is the house playing Simon Says?"

Then something new happened. A speaker crackled.

"Hello."

Another speaker answered from the kitchen.

"Hello."

Then the hallway speaker.

"Hello."

The voice activated speakers were acting weird.

Codey covered his ears and laughed.

"Okay, okay! I heard you!"

"Stop," Codey said.

The speaker kept talking.

Cypher watched the blinking lights.

"They copy what they hear," she said.

"They repeat what they see."

The house glowed faint green.

"That's how a swarm of zombie bots begins."

"Sometimes," Cypher said,

"something outside the house sends them the same instructions."

"They're not broken," Cypher said.

"When many devices follow the same instructions together, it's called a botnet."

"Like echoes," she added.

The doorbell rang.

No one was there.

The smart fridge hummed.

The thermostat clicked.

The robot vacuum rolled forward,

then stopped. It wasn't connecting to the internet.

Codey pressed the remote.

"We didn't invite you," Codey told the vacuum.

Nothing happened.

Codey stared.

"Why is everything acting the same silly way?"

Some things joined the swarm faster than others.

An old toy blinked without stopping.

A dusty speaker crackled too long.

Cypher pointed gently.

"Some things don't slow down," she said.

"They don't stop to check if something feels wrong."

Codey frowned.

"Like running without looking?"

Cypher nodded.

"And that makes them easier to pull along."

Every light turned on.

All at once.

The TV froze.

The smart devices kept losing connection.

The doorbell rang again.

The house waited, stuck listening to itself.

Codey flipped the smart light switch.

Nothing.

"It's busy," he said.

Codey laughed nervously.

"I think my house is confused."

The house was so busy talking to itself that nothing listened anymore.

Codey stared at the lights.

“Helpful alone,” Cypher said.

“Dangerous together.”

Codey nodded slowly.

“That’s the danger of swarms.”

“When everything talks at once,” Cypher said,

“someone else gets to decide what they do.”

The lights didn't turn off.

But they stopped blinking together.

One paused.

Another waited.

The speaker said "Hello,"

then stayed quiet.

Codey blinked.

"Did it just... hesitate?"

The house still felt strange.

But not stuck.

The TV flickered,

then showed a picture.

The doorbell stayed quiet.

Cypher nodded.

"Less copying," she said with a smile.

"More listening."

Codey frowned.

"So... do we stop it?"

Cypher shook her head gently.

"Stopping one device won't help," she said.

She gestured around the room.

"This isn't one thing.

"It's many small things being told what to do together."

She smiled softly.

"That's called a botnet."

Codey looked again.

Not at the lights.

Not at the screens.

But at the pauses between them.

"They're not copying anymore," Codey said slowly.

"They've stopped listening to the signal."

Cypher nodded softly.

"When they stopped copying," she said,

"they stopped listening to the wrong signal."

Everything slowed.

Almost stopped.

The green glow softened.

Codey took a breath.

And waited.

The light turned on

when Codey flipped the switch.

The speaker stayed quiet

until someone spoke.

Codey smiled.

“It’s listening again,” Codey said.

The house was still connected.

Still smart.

Still full of helpful things.

Just... calmer.

Cypher smiled.

"You didn't fight it," she said.

"You understood how it was being used."

Codey looked around his room.

Everything felt normal again.

"It didn't need fixing," he said quietly.

"It needed better choices."

Cypher nodded.

"And those start small."

Codey smiled.

"We learn from the past," he said.

"Protect the present."

He paused.

"And shape the future."

The
Cyber Ghost Crew!

Who is Codey?

Codey is a curious kid just like you. Sometimes homework feels boring, until it turns into an adventure.

What makes Codey special?

- **He asks questions**
- **He learns from mistakes**
- **He gets braver with every mission**

Codey's Rule: "If I don't understand it yet, I will soon."

Fun Fact: Codey doesn't defeat cyber threats with strength. He wins by learning and thinking smart.

Who is Cypher?

Cypher is a Time-Travel Defender of the Digital Realm.

She protects the past, present, and future of technology.

What does Cypher do?
- Guides others through making better cyber decisions
- Explains big cyber ideas in simple ways
- Keeps missions on track when things get dangerous

Cypher's Rule: "Knowledge is the strongest defense."

Fun Fact: Cypher doesn't fight threats directly. She helps others learn how to stop them.

The ChronoCipher hourglass

The ChronoCipher is Cypher's powerful hourglass.

What's inside? Along with sand, it holds glowing 1s and 0s (binary!)

What does it do?

- Lets Cypher travel to the Digital Realm
- Pulses and dims when cyber mistakes are being made
- Only stops glowing when the lesson is learned

⭐ REMEMBER ⭐

Core Lesson of Book 5: Resilience and control

Every device matters.

Somewhere else, far from glowing cities and steady signals...

A cat stretched, yawned, and tapped a screen with his paw.

A warning blinked.

Clix didn't read it.

He clicked.

And somewhere—

Cypher felt the ChronoCipher stir.

Made in the USA
Monee, IL
05 November 2026

67380076R00029